POWWOW

Festivals and Holidays

By June Behrens

Photographs compiled by Terry Behrens

 CHILDRENS PRESS, CHICAGO

TO BLANCHE BREWSTER

ACKNOWLEDGMENTS

The author wishes to acknowledge with thanks the assistance of Eva North-rup, called Seyweemana, of the Hopi Indian tribe. Ms. Northrup serves as project manager of EONA, Educational Opportunities for Native Americans, in the Long Beach Unified School District, Long Beach, California. A special thanks to Dan James of the Choctaw tribe, teacher in the Long Beach Unified School District.

PHOTO CREDITS

David Tuch: COVER photograph
          Selected scenes
Elyn Marton: Selected scenes

Library of Congress Cataloging in Publication Data

Behrens, June.
  Powwow.

  (Festivals and holidays)
  Summary: Describes a visit to a powwow, or Native American celebration, where American Indian families get together to enjoy traditional food, music, dancing, and crafts.
  1. Indians of North America—Rites and ceremonies—Juvenile literature.
[1. Indians of North America—Rites and ceremonies. 2. Festivals] I. Behrens, Terry, ill. II. Title. III. Series.
E98.R3B285 1983   394.2′68′08997   83-7274
ISBN 0-516-02387-X

Listen to the drums! They are the heartbeat of the Powwow. The dancers move faster and faster. They keep perfect time with the beat of the drums.

Our friend Red Elk has invited us
to the Powwow. In school, Red Elk
is called Billy.

The Powwow is a special gathering
for Native American families. Native
Americans are descendants of Indians
who lived in America before the
early settlers came.

Red Elk tells us the Powwow is
an American Indian ceremony and
tribal custom. Sometimes it is called
a Tribal Fair or an Indian Days
Festival. It might celebrate a special
date, or just be a time to get
together for fun. Powwow is a grand
picnic with food and singing and
drums and dancing!

The Powwow pulls tribes and
families together. It brings pride and
harmony into their hearts. At the
Powwow the elders pass on the old
ways, or traditions, to the young.
Indian dancers follow in the steps of
their ancestors. The songs have been
sung by many generations.

Skills at games and storytelling
are passed from parents to children,
as are tribal arts and crafts.

Red Elk takes us to see his uncle,
Good Eagle, the pipe maker. Good
Eagle greets us with *hau, wakanyeja.*
This means "Hello, children" in the
Sioux language.

8

Good Eagle tells us the Powwow may be small, with just a few families. Or, it could be a large gathering, with thousands of people coming from many tribes and many states. Those who come from far away bring campers and vans. Sometimes they may even pitch their teepees!

At the Powwow the Native Americans might speak English or the language of their tribe. There are many tribes and many languages.

Good Eagle says the contests are an important part of the Powwow. Who will be chosen the best dancers and singers? Everyone wants to know.

The fancy dancers wear beautiful
costumes of feathers and beads. They
paint their faces and bodies. The
designs might be passed down from
one generation to another. Dancers
spend hours getting ready for
contests.

This Powwow will last for one
day. Others might last for four or
five days. Many Powwows are held
each year in various parts of the
United States.

This Powwow is in a park. Some
Powwows are held on fairgrounds
and farms or on Indian reservations.
Often a rodeo and crafts fair are
part of the Powwow.

Red Elk wants us to try the fry
bread. It's his favorite. Fry bread
looks like a large pancake sprinkled
with powdered sugar. Is it good!

Red Elk reminds us that Native
Americans have given us many gifts
of food. Long ago they cultivated
wild plants. Today we enjoy corn,
potatoes, beans, tomatoes, and many
other foods first grown by Indian
farmers long ago. We can thank
them for popcorn, peanuts, and
chewing gum, too.

Red Elk shows us a sand painting. We watch the artist sprinkle colored sand into the design. The design may be a god or a sacred symbol used many times before.

Red Elk says that once sand painting was used by the elders for healing. If someone were ill, a sand painting was made in a day and destroyed before sunset. Many people believed the sand took away the cause of the illness.

Look at the beautiful beads and
jewelry! Red Elk tells us that Indians
know which tribe made the jewelry
by the patterns in the work. Native
American jewelry is made from seeds,
bones, feathers, and shells. Stones,
such as turquoise and coral, are set in
silver by skilled silversmiths.

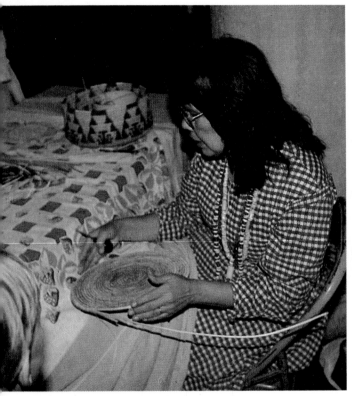

Making baskets, rugs, and blankets
are weaving skills passed from mother
to daughter. The elders are eager for
the young people to carry on their
work as artists.

What is the game those children
are playing? It's called "hunt the
stones." We run all over the park to
find the stones!

Red Elk shows us how to play a
guessing game. He has a bone hidden
in each hand. One bone is plain and
the other is marked. We must try to
guess which hand holds the
unmarked bone.

These are the same games played
by Indian children long ago.

Red Elk tells us about the Kachina doll. It represents Kachina spirits, or supernatural beings. They are the mythical ancestors of the Pueblo people. Kachina spirits might bring plentiful crops or gifts for the children.

Indians believed in the spirit forces in nature. They believed animals and plants, as well as the sun, wind, and rain, had spirits just like people. Disasters were caused by evil or angered spirits.

Miracle workers, called medicine men, were supposed to have power to influence spirit forces. Many modern Indians still practice these beliefs.

We know that Red Elk's ancestors were the first people in America. They explored and cultivated the land long before the settlers came from Europe.

In each region of America there were many tribes and many cultures. The woodland Indians lived in the eastern forests. The plains Indians were the hunters, and roamed over the Midwest's grassy plains.

The shepherds of the Southwest
herded animals, and the farmers
planted crops. The seed gatherers of
the West were wanderers, and the
Northwest Indians were fishermen.
Red Elk and his family are from the
Sioux tribe. In early times his people
were plains Indians.

As our nation grew, the settlers
moved to new places. The land
where Indians had lived was taken
by white men. Many Indians were
sent from their homes to Indian
Territory. The lands reserved for
Indians became reservations.
Reservations were public lands set
aside by the United States
government as homes for Native
Americans.

Good Eagle tells us that in 1924 Native Americans were made citizens. Many are citizens of their Indian nation tribes as well as United States citizens.

There are about 1.5 million Indians in the United States. Over half of them no longer live on reservations. They live in cities and towns in all parts of America.

California is called the Indian
capital because this state has the
most Indians living in it. More than
200,000 Indians from many tribes
live in California.

Red Elk and his family often go to
the Indian Center. Here they can
meet their friends and keep alive
respect and pride for the old ways of
the elders. The Indian Center helps
to organize Powwows and brings
people together from all the tribes.

Here come the dancers again!
Listen to the music. Drums and
rattles, whistles and flutes are the
music makers. They make the rhythm
for the singers and dancers.

These dances are for fun and show.
Let's see who is best. All ages dance,
from the very young to the skilled
men's fancy dancers.

Each dance has a meaning. Some dancers imitate animal and bird movements. Others tell stories of events in the lives of the people.

Long ago, dances were for religious or magical reasons, too. Indians danced to heal the sick, to bring rain, or to make the corn grow. There were special dances for the buffalo hunt. Other dances told the history of the tribe. Sometimes the costumes help us to understand what the dance is about.

We thank Red Elk and Good Eagle for sharing their Powwow. We have eaten fry bread and watched the craftsmen. We have heard the drums and swayed with the painted dancers. We have listened to the singers and played the games. We have become a part of the Powwow spirit.

We say *ake wancinyankin kte*. In the Sioux language this means "We'll see you again, at the next Powwow!"

Epilogue

All life that is holy and good for we two-leggeds
is shared with the four-leggeds
and the wings of the air
and all green things; for these are children
of one mother
and their father is one spirit.

Black Elk

Powwow is a social gathering for Native Americans. It pulls tribes and extended families together and unites them in a revival of Indian pride.

Powwow reflects one aspect of Indian life as it is today, within the framework of ceremonies and traditions, music and dance, arts and crafts.

We glimpse the history of a people and learn about their early beliefs and cultural contributions. We are brought into scenes that capture the spirit of Powwow and bring us to a better understanding of our Native American friends and neighbors.

Powwow gives us a feeling for the underlying thread of the old and the new in today's society.

JUNE BEHRENS has written more than fifty books, plays, and filmstrips for young people, touching on all subject areas of the school curriculum. *Powwow* is the third book in the Festivals and Holidays Series. Mrs. Behrens has for many years been an educator in one of California's largest public school systems. She is a graduate of the University of California at Santa Barbara and has a Master's degree from the University of Southern California. Mrs. Behrens is listed in *Who's Who of American Women*. She is a recipient of the Distinguished Alumni Award from the University of California for her contributions in the field of education. She and her husband live in Rancho Palos Verdes, a Southern California suburb.

TERRY BEHRENS has compiled the photographs for three books in the Festivals and Holidays Series. Ms. Behrens is a photographer and a teacher of English as a Second Language in the California public schools. She is a graduate of California Polytechnic University and has studied at the University of London and Universidad de Morelos in Mexico.

DAVID TUCH is a retired businessman, philanthropist, and professional photographer. His work as a photographer has won international acclaim. A one man show in Hong Kong earned him a life membership in the Chinese Photographic Society. His photography has been featured in *Westways*, *People's Almanac*, and other prominent publications. His work was displayed in the Fine Arts Pavillion of the 1982 World's Fair, and is on permanent exhibit at Skirball Museum in Los Angeles.